The Ballerina and the Clown

Contents

About *The Ballerina and the Clown*

Hans Christian Andersen (1805–75) was not only a great writer but a great master of papercutting (or "cutting out," as it is called in the United States), one of those near-universal domestic arts practiced at one time or another by virtually every schoolchild. Andersen's papercuts are much like his tales: intricate, surprising, sometimes caustically funny, and far more powerful than their humble scale might suggest. *The Ballerina and the Clown* develops a completely new story (although readers of Andersen's tales will recognize several familiar themes) from eight of Anderson's most charming papercuts, which are reproduced in the score.

First performance: 5 May 2002, Hendricks Chapel, Syracuse University, Syracuse, New York, by the Syracuse Children's Chorus, Barbara M. Tagg, conductor, and Grace Wong, harp.

I.
The Clown

Upon a time a dancing girl,
a girl atwirl, once loved a clown.
She loved him up, she loved him down.
She loved his sad and silly face,
his lanky neck, his awkward grace.
And he loved her: oh what a girl
to keep him in a happy whirl!

Commissioned by the Syracuse Children's Chorus, Barbara M. Tagg, conductor,
with funds from the National Endowment for the Arts

THE BALLERINA AND THE CLOWN

A Hans Christian Andersen Tale
For Children's Chorus (SAA) and Harp

Sally M. Gall

Libby Larsen

1. The Clown

2.
The Clown Goes To Visit His Ballerina

"Swan, swan, get out of my way,
I'm off to visit my love today.

I'll take her my garland of flowers sweet,
and I won't let you nibble my flowers or feet.

Swan, swan, get out of my way,
I'm off to visit my love today."

2. The Clown Goes To Visit His Ballerina

Soprano: "Swan,— swan,— get

Alto: "Swan,— swan,— swan,— swan,— get

out of my way, I'm off to vis-it my love to-day.

out of my way, I'm off to vis-it my love to-day.

I'll take her my gar-land of flo-wers sweet and I

I'll take her my gar-land of flo-wers sweet, and I

*Harmonics written where played.

won't let you nib-ble my flowers or feet. Swan,—

won't let you nib-ble my flo-wers or —feet. Swan,— swan,—

swan,— get out of my way, I'm off to vis-it my love to-day.

swan,— swan,— get out of my way, I'm off to vis-it my love to-day.

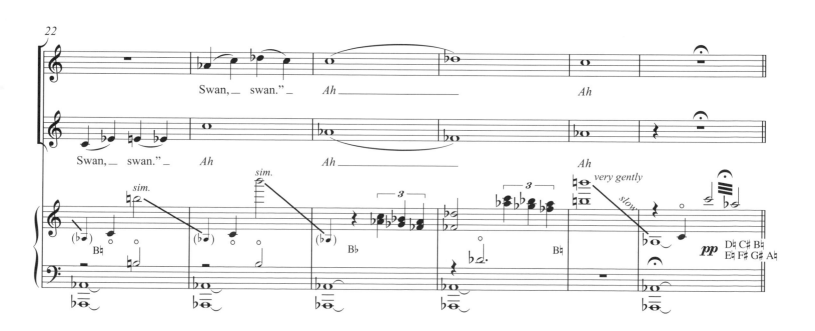

Swan,— swan."— Ah ———————— Ah

Swan,— swan."— Ah ———— Ah ———————— Ah

3.

The Clown Arrives At the Theater

"Doorkeeper, doorkeeper, is my darling here?"

Your darling is who? Who would love you?

"The prettiest girl who dances for you,
she can dance all day, and all night too."

*We had such a girl, but she's gone away.
Where she is now. I cannot say.*

3. The Clown Arrives At the Theater

*Use a character voice for the Doorkeeper's throughout this section.

4.
The Sandman Sends Him a Dream

The clown searched high,
the clown searched low.
"Where oh where did my darling go?"
Poor clown, poor clown.

He asked whomever he did meet
"Where is my girl with the dancing feet?"
Poor clown, poor clown.

Winter came and bitter cold.
Each night he prayed, "God keep her warm,"
Poor clown, poor clown.

One night as he lay asleep,
the sandman sent him a dream to keep.

He thought he walked in a lovely place,
soft breezes blowing against his face.

The sky and sea were bright and blue,
and flowers blossomed in every hue.

There high up in a slim palm tree
his girl was dancing happily.
Poor clown, poor clown.

"Oh blessèd dream: for by the sea
I know my darling waits for me.
I will search most patiently
and bring her home by skate and ski."
Poor clown, poor clown.

4. The Sandman Sends Him a Dream

He asked whom - ev - er he did meet,

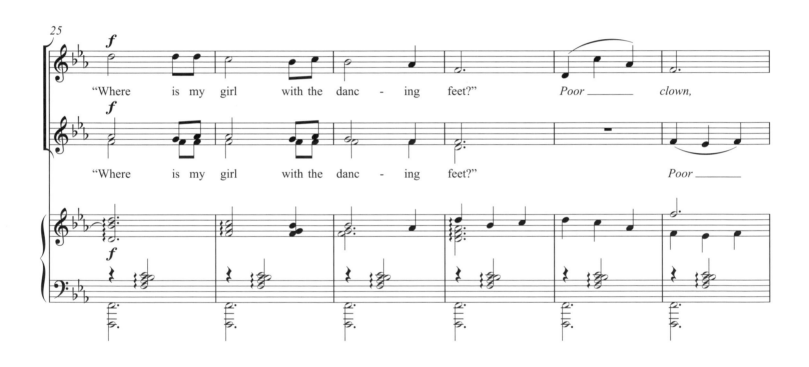

"Where is my girl with the danc - ing feet?" Poor _____ clown,

"Where is my girl with the danc - ing feet?" Poor _____

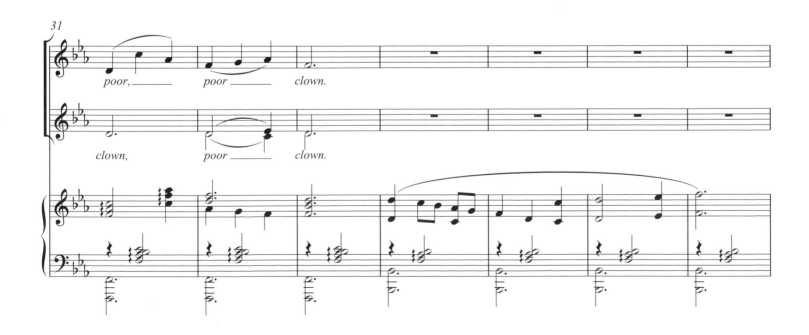

poor, _____ poor _____ clown.

clown, poor _____ clown.

Win-ter came and bit-ter cold. Each night he prayed,___

oo ___ *oo* ___

SPEAKER: One night as he lay asleep, the sandman sent him a dream to keep.

"God keep her warm." — *Poor* *clown,* *poor* _ *clown.* _

Poor _ *clown,* _ *poor* _ *clown.* _ *Poor* _ *clown,* _ *poor* _

He thought he walked in a lovely place, soft breezes blowing against his face. There high up in a slim palm tree his girl

Poor *clown,* *poor* _ *clown.* _ *Poor* *clown,* *poor* _

5.

A Message From the Storks

"Beware of Sunflower Man, we say,
he steals hearts both night and day!"

5. A Message From the Storks

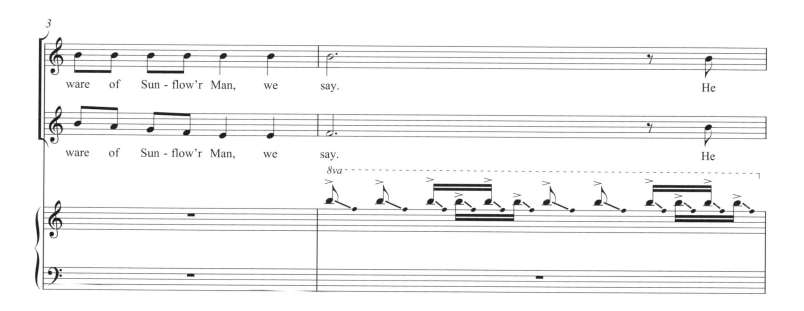

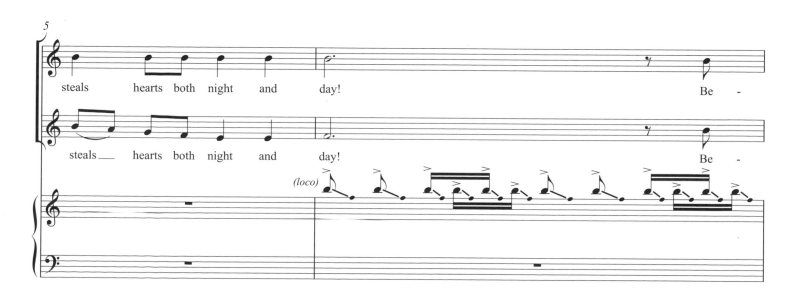

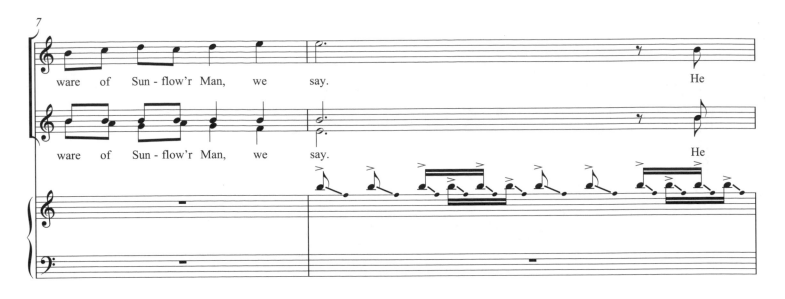

ware of Sun - flow'r Man, we say. He

ware of Sun - flow'r Man, we say. He

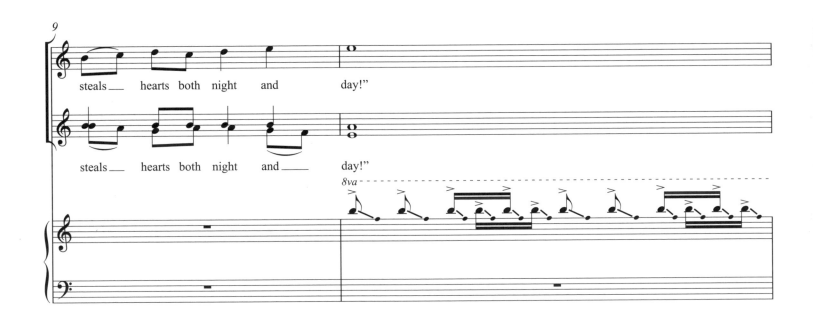

steals___ hearts both night and day!"

steals___ hearts both night and ___ day!"

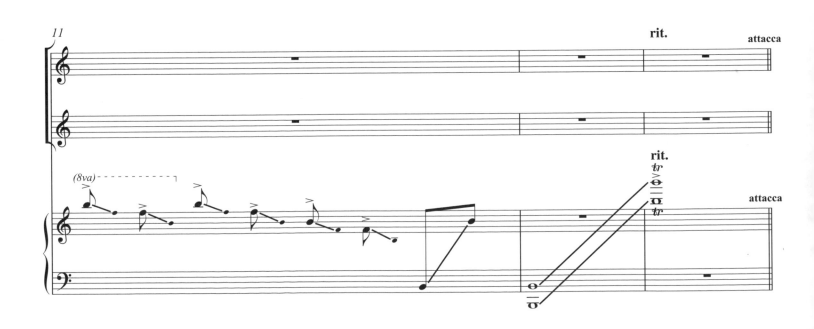

rit.

attacca

6.
The Clown Finds His Way South

The clown walked south through ice and snow,
his warm heart told him where to go.

He came to a kind and pleasant land
by a bright-blue sea with golden sand.

Here scarlet pomegranates and laurel trees
rustled their leaves in the gentle breeze.

Young boys and girls danced hand in hand,
oranges and lemons smelled so grand.

He followed a crowd to the market place,
what he saw then, made his poor heart race.

Up on a stage was his dancing girl,
and Sunflower Man was making her whirl.

6. The Clown Finds His Way South

land   by   a   bright - blue   sea   with __ gold - en   sand.

blue ____ sea   with __ gold - en   sand.

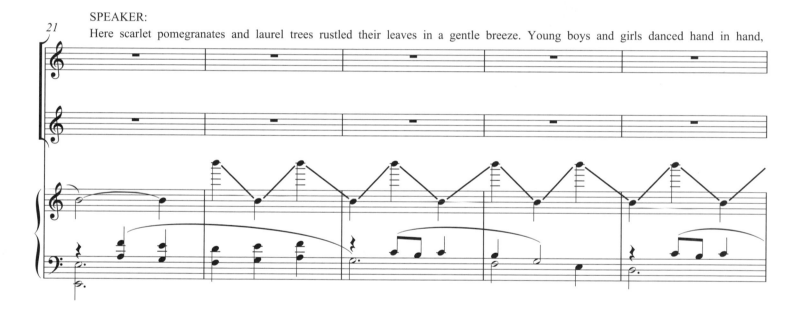

SPEAKER:
Here scarlet pomegranates and laurel trees rustled their leaves in a gentle breeze. Young boys and girls danced hand in hand,

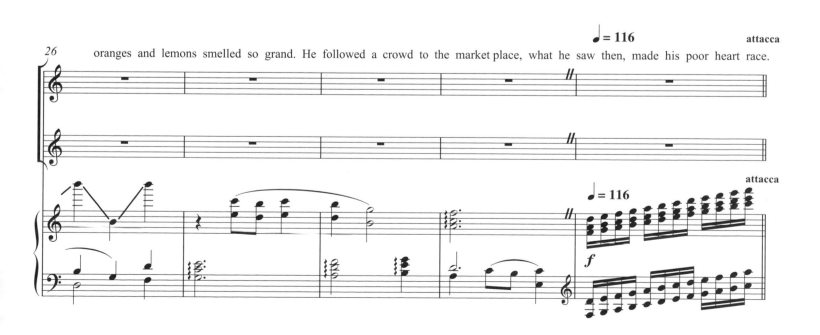

♩ = 116   attacca

oranges and lemons smelled so grand. He followed a crowd to the market place, what he saw then, made his poor heart race.

♩ = 116

attacca

7.

Sunflower Man Shows Off the Ballerina

"Friends, friends, friends, come gather round,
look at the dancing toy I found.

She can dance and twirl up on her toes,
and the faster I clap, the faster she goes.

Faster, girl, turn into a blur,
or I'll goad you with my golden spur.

Faster, girl, dance, hop, and skip,
or with my whip I'll make you trip."

Then the clown called his darling's name aloud
and somersaulted right through the crowd.

He flew upon the stage with a backwards flip
and ran with his girl to a little ship.

Soon they docked in the northern sea,
and he took her home by skate and ski.

Now when the storks look down they see
a girl and clown dance happily.

7. Sunflower Man Shows Off the Ballerina

She can dance and twirl up on her toes,_____ and the

She can dance and twirl up on her toes,_____ and the

fast-er I clap the fast - er she goes.

fast-er I clap the fast - er she goes.

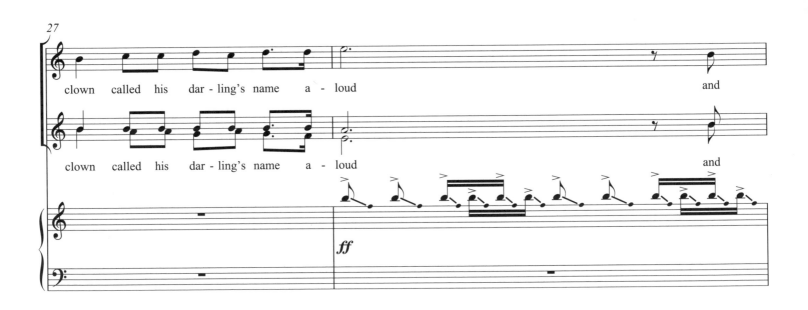

He flew up-on the stage with a back - ward

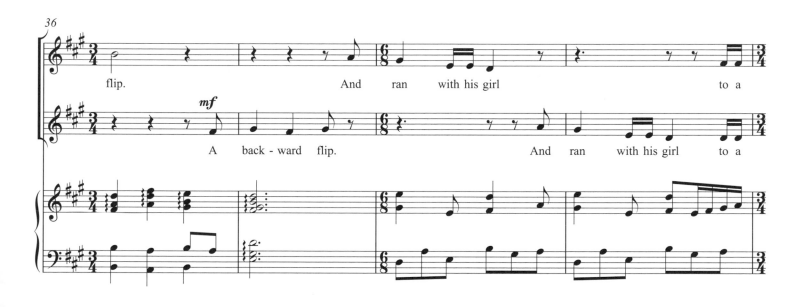

flip. And ran with his girl to a

A back - ward flip. And ran with his girl to a

lit - tle ship.

lit - tle ship.

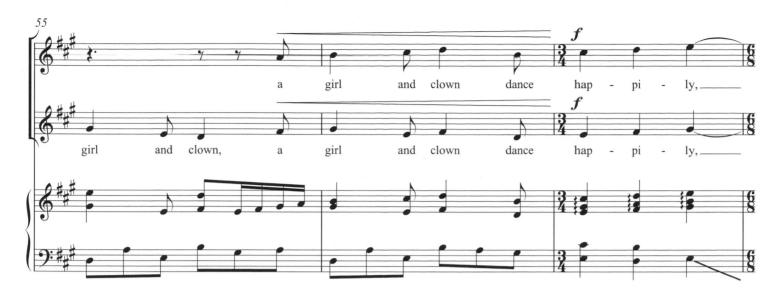

a girl and clown dance hap - pi - ly, _____

girl and clown, a girl and clown dance hap - pi - ly, _____

_____ a girl and clown dance

_____ a girl and clown dance

hap - - - - - - - pi - ly.

hap - - - - - - - pi - ly.

Illustration used by permission of the Odense Bys Museer.